W9-CGX-297

ANDERSON

LIFE CYCLES

The
Frog

Copyright © 1997 Steck-Vaughn Company

All rights reserved. No part of this book may be reproduced or utilized in any form or by any means, electronic or mechanical, including photocopying, recording, or by any information storage and retrieval system, without permission in writing from the Publisher. Inquiries should be addressed to: Copyright Permissions, Steck-Vaughn Company, P.O. Box 26015, Austin, TX 78755.

Published by Raintree Steck-Vaughn Publishers, an imprint of Steck-Vaughn Company.

Acknowledgments
Project Editor: Helene Resky
Design Manager: Joyce Spicer
Consulting Editor: Kim Merlino
Consultant: Michael Chinery
Illustrated by Colin Newman
Designed by Ian Winton and Steve Prosser
Electronic Cover Production: Alan Klemp
Additional Electronic Production: Bo McKinney and Scott Melcer
Photography credits on page 32

Planned and produced by The Creative Publishing Company

Library of Congress Cataloging-in-Publication Data
    Crewe, Sabrina
    The frog / Sabrina Crewe.
       p.   cm. — (Life cycles)
    Includes index.
    Summary: Describes the habitat, eating habits, and life cycle of frogs.
    ISBN 0-8172-4369-0 (hardcover). — ISBN 0-8172-6232-6 (pbk.)
    1. Frogs — Juvenile literature.   2. Rana pipiens — Juvenile literature.   3. Frogs — Life cycles — Juvenile literature.   4. Rana pipiens — Life cycles — Juvenile literature.
[1. Northern leopard frog.   2. Frogs.]   I. Title.   II. Series: Crewe, Sabrina. Life cycles.
QL668.E27C74   1997
597.8 — dc20   96-4831
                                                     CIP   AC

1 2 3 4 5 6 7 8 9 0 LB 00 99 98 97 96
Printed and bound in the United States of America.

Words explained in the glossary appear in **bold** the first time they are used in the text.

The
Frog

Sabrina Crewe

RSVP

**RAINTREE
STECK-VAUGHN**
P U B L I S H E R S
The Steck-Vaughn Company

Austin, Texas

The frogs' eggs are in the water.

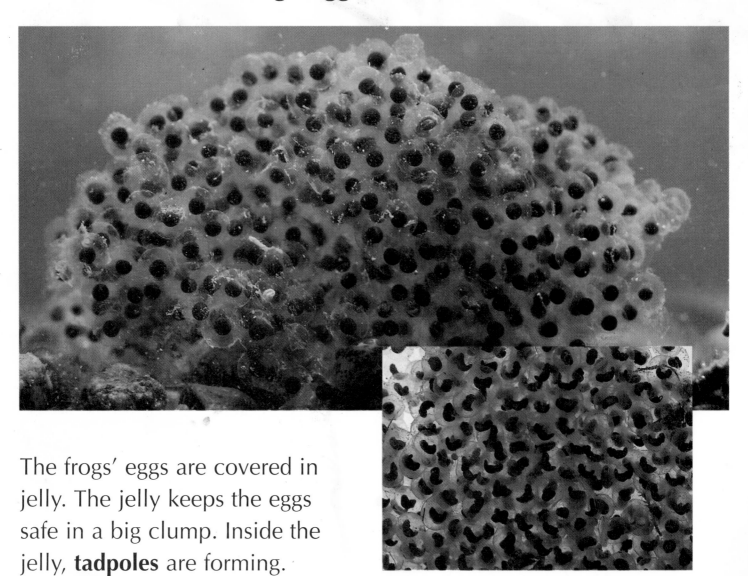

The frogs' eggs are covered in jelly. The jelly keeps the eggs safe in a big clump. Inside the jelly, **tadpoles** are forming.

4

The tadpoles hatch from the jelly.

After two or three weeks, the tadpoles are ready to **hatch**. They wriggle their way out of the jelly.

The tadpoles stick to the jelly.

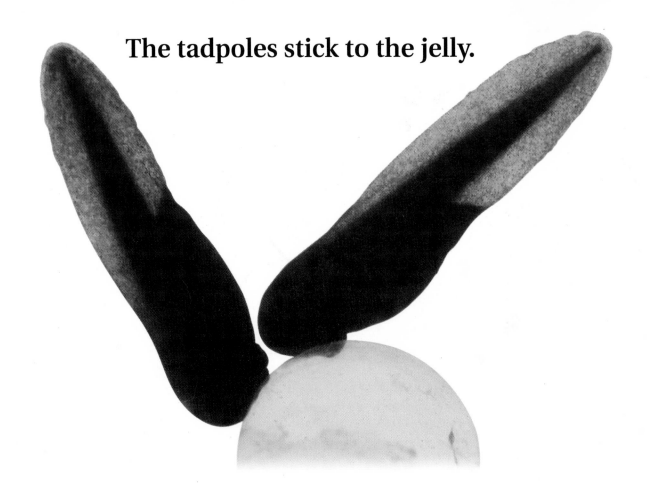

When tadpoles hatch, they cling onto the jelly with their **suckers**. After a few days, the tadpoles leave the jelly and start to look for food in the pond.

Tadpoles breathe under the water.

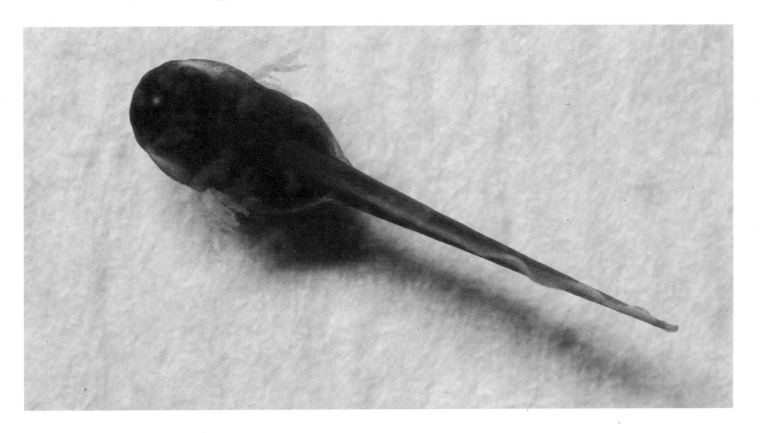

The tadpole has **gills** on each side of its body. The tadpole uses its gills to breathe. Soon the tadpole will breathe with new gills inside its body.

The tadpoles are looking for food.

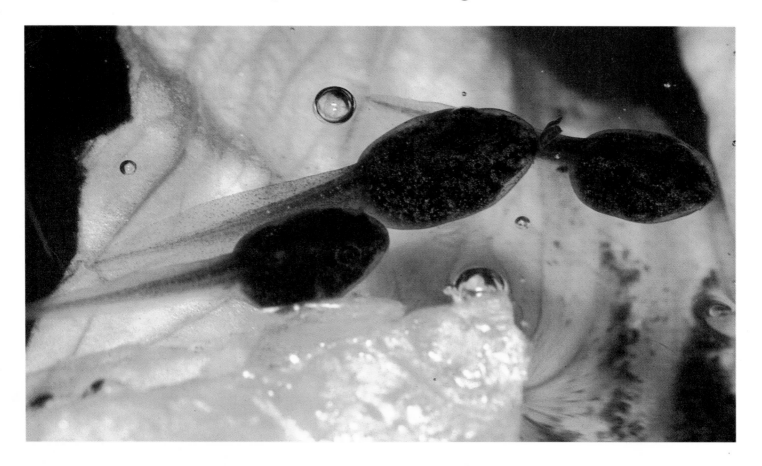

The tadpoles are two weeks old. They
have started to eat plants growing in
the water. They can also eat tiny animals.

The tadpole has grown legs!

Tadpoles start to grow back legs when they are five weeks old. As the legs grow, five toes appear on each foot. The tadpole's toes are webbed and make good paddles in the water.

The tadpole comes up for air.

The tadpole has grown **lungs** inside its body. It doesn't use gills to breathe anymore. The tadpole reaches above the water with its mouth. It breathes air through its mouth and into its new lungs.

The tadpole is getting bigger.

The tadpole has changed again.
It has little front legs. Its body is
growing fast.

The tadpole looks like a frog!

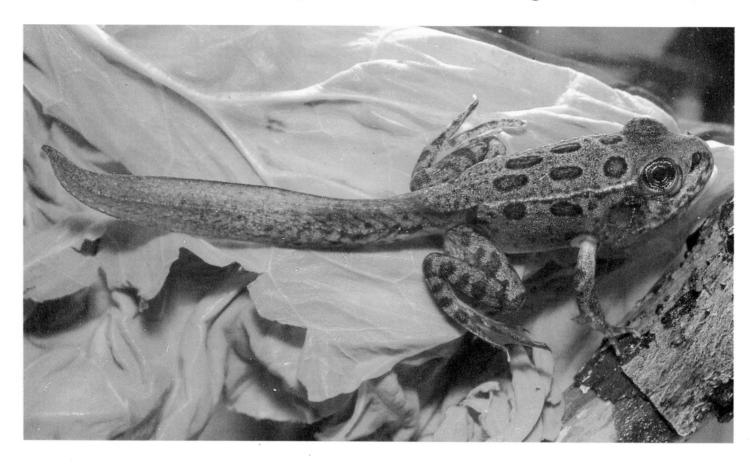

The legs of the tadpole get bigger and
stronger every day. Its tail is getting smaller.
Soon it won't be a tadpole anymore.

The frog hops out of the pond.

When it is three months old, the little frog is ready to get out of the water. At first it stays close to the pond, sitting on a leaf.

The frog has found a worm.

Frogs eat small animals, such as
spiders, worms, and insects. The frog
can hold slippery worms with the
tiny teeth around its mouth.

The frog has a sticky tongue.

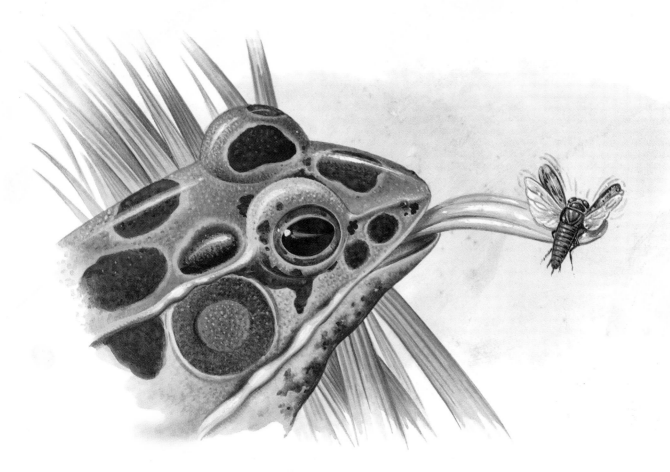

The frog's tongue is very long. It pops out
quickly to catch insects. The insects stick
to the frog's tongue and are swallowed.

The frog is pulling off its skin!

Frogs **molt** a few times every year.
When the old skin begins to split, the
frog pulls it off with its feet. There is
a new, soft skin under the old skin.

The frog's skin helps it hide.

Frogs can make their skin get darker or lighter to match the place they are in. This is called **camouflage**. Frogs camouflage themselves when they need to hide.

The snake is dangerous.

Frogs have many **predators**.
Turtles and fish catch frogs in
the water. Snakes, birds, and
bigger animals try to catch
frogs when they are on land.

The frog leaps out of danger!

The frog's legs are very strong. The
frog can leap far on land or jump
high out of water. This is how
it escapes from predators.

Winter is coming.

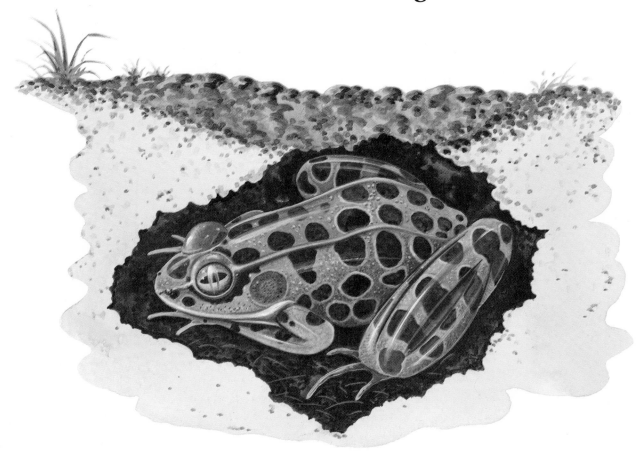

When it gets cold, frogs hide in the mud or go under a stone. They stay very quiet and still. Frogs **hibernate** until the spring.

The frog comes out of the mud.

Spring is here. The frog has woken up.
It is ready to go back to its pond.

The frogs gather together.

The frogs have arrived at their pond.
Some have traveled from a few miles
away. The male frogs arrive before the
female frogs.

Male frogs are very noisy!

Male frogs make noise by puffing out their **vocal sacs**. They do this to call the female frogs to the pond.

The female frog is full of eggs.

The female frog is ready to mate with a
male frog. She needs to lay her eggs. The
male frog will **fertilize** the eggs when she
releases them into the water.

Frogs need wet places.

Frogs need to live near water that is clean and full of living things. Many ponds have been **polluted**. People can help frogs by keeping ponds and other wet places safe for plants and animals.

Parts of a Frog

Frogs are **amphibians**. Most amphibians start their life in water. When they are grown, they can live on land and in water. Some amphibians live only in water. A few live only on land, usually in wet places.

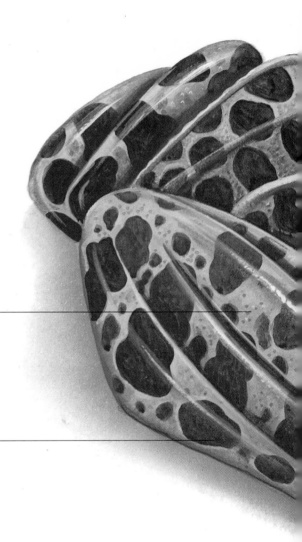

Skin
Takes in water so there is no need to drink

Back legs
Very long and strong for leaping and swimming

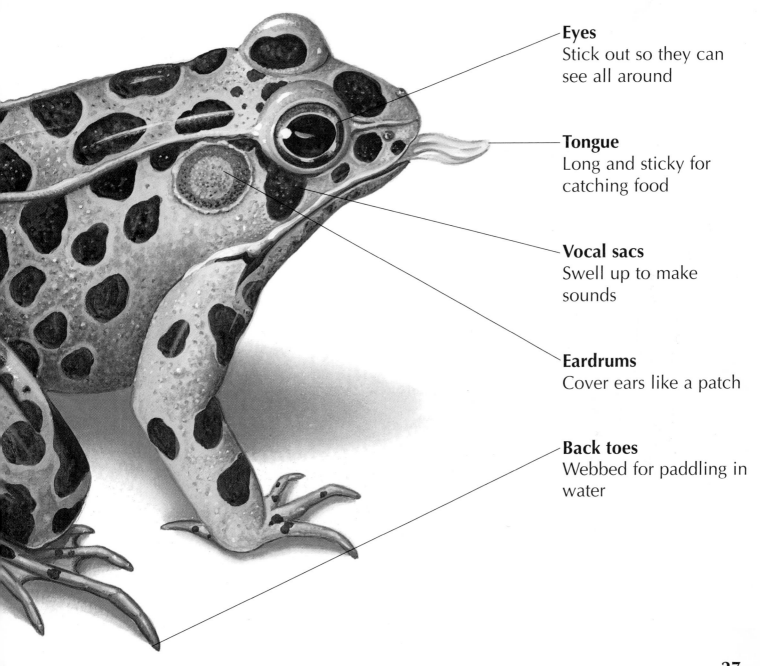

Eyes
Stick out so they can see all around

Tongue
Long and sticky for catching food

Vocal sacs
Swell up to make sounds

Eardrums
Cover ears like a patch

Back toes
Webbed for paddling in water

Other Amphibians

The frog in this book is a northern leopard frog. Here are some other frogs and different kinds of amphibians.

Green tree frog

Pacific giant salamander

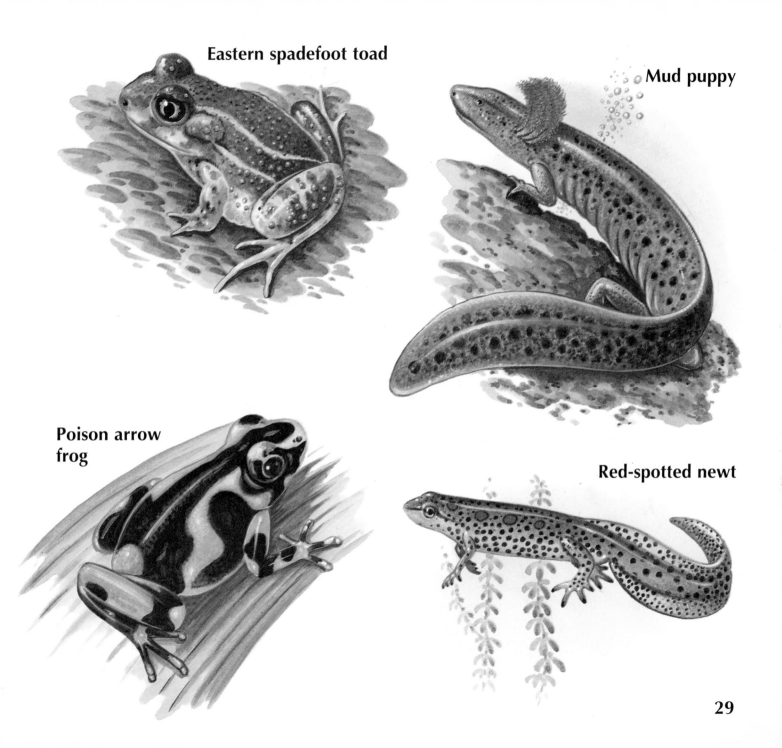

Eastern spadefoot toad

Mud puppy

Poison arrow frog

Red-spotted newt

Where the Northern Leopard Frog Lives

Alaska

CANADA

UNITED
STATES

Areas where
the northern
leopard frog
lives

MEXICO

Glossary

Amphibian A kind of animal that lives and breathes in water when it is young but lives and breathes on land as an adult

Camouflage A way of hiding something against its background

Fertilize To make a female's eggs able to produce babies

Gills Parts of an animal's body that are used for breathing in water

Hatch To come out at birth

Hibernate To spend winter in a deep sleep

Lungs Parts of an animal's body that are used for breathing in air

Molt To shed hair, skin, or feathers when they are worn and need replacing

Pollute To make something dirty

Predator An animal that hunts and kills other animals for food

Sucker A body part that can stick to something else by sucking

Tadpole The growing stage in the life of a frog before it becomes an adult

Vocal sacs The parts of a frog that it uses to make sounds

Index

Photography credits

Front cover: (top left) Gregory K. Scott/Photo Researchers/Oxford Scientific Films; (middle left) John Mitchell/Oxford Scientific Films; (bottom left) Stephen Dalton/Oxford Scientific Films; (right) S. L. and J. T. Collins/Photo Researchers/Oxford Scientific Films.

Title page: John Netherton/Oxford Scientific Films; p. 4: (top) Gregory K. Scott/Photo Researchers/Oxford Scientific Films; (bottom) John Mitchell/ Oxford Scientific Films; p. 5: R. Austing/FLPA; pp. 6 & 7: Harry Rogers/ Photo Researchers/Oxford Scientific Films; pp. 8-13: John Mitchell/ Oxford Scientific Films; p. 14: John Mitchell/Photo Researchers/Oxford Scientific Films; p. 17: Rod Planck/Dembinsky Photo Assoc./FLPA; p. 18: Breck P. Kent/Animals Animals/Oxford Scientific Films; p. 19: Stephen Dalton/Oxford Scientific Films; p. 21: Ed Wolff/Animals Animals/ Oxford Scientific Films; p. 23: Zig Leszczynski/Animals Animals/Oxford Scientific Films; p. 24: John Mitchell/Oxford Scientific Films; p. 25: Christine M. Douglas/Photo Researchers/Oxford Scientific Films.